PRINCIPLES FOR THE PURPOSED MAN

Practical Applied-Principles for Men in Pursuit of Purpose

Archie T. Smith, Th.M.,
Pastor, Spread the Word Worship Center NC
Fayetteville, North Carolina

Principles for the Purposed Man
Practical Applied-Principles for Men in Pursuit of Purpose

Archie T. Smith, Th.M.
Pastor, Spread the Word Worship Center NC

Table of Contents

Introduction
Why Men?
Why Proverbs?
How to Use This Book

Proverbial Principles

Principle 1 – Begin with Reverence
Principle 2 – Make a Conscious Effort to Avoid the Seductive
Principle 3 – Trust Dictates Trajectory
Principle 4 – Do Discipline!
Principle 5 – Force Yourself to Remain "In-Gear"
Principle 6 – Discover and Develop Your Gift
Principle 7 – Correct Your Company
Principle 8 – Do Not Hate on Them
Principle 9 – Remember HIS Sovereignty
Principle 10 – Show Honor

A Prayer for Purpose

Introduction

Why Men?

We choose to write toward the universal purpose as well as to the individual purpose that God has specifically designed for each Man, because, simply put, the enemy is trying to attack them at a higher clout. Satan has one purpose, "steal, kill, and destroy," (John 10:10). The enemy has discovered that if he can destroy a man and his purpose, he can destroy everything that he comes into contact with.

It is a very strategic way to destroy marriages, families, friendships, businesses, communities, churches, and ultimately nations and kingdoms. The man is a target because of the weight of authority God placed into each of their hands. It began with Adam, God gave him extreme levels of authority and the enemy attempted to rob him of it and everything connected to it by deceiving him. It was a subtle attack that would affect generations and if we as men, are not able to escape and withstand the tactics of the enemy in pursuit of our purpose, generations will be affected.

We are seeing that very principle manifested across the country even today. The tactics of the enemy are destroying generations of families on a daily basis. If you haven't checked the statistics of fatherless homes and their affects alone, you would be surprisingly appalled. It is devastating!

Therefore, men need encouragement from other men who have made mistakes, poor decisions, and experienced hardship, but never gave up and, thanks to God's grace, have come back VICTORIOUS and more set upon purpose than ever. Men are significant. Men are struggling. Men are unique. Men are important and even more important to God!

Why Proverbs?

One of the many pitfalls of men is that, although their father of parental role model gave them wise advice, they often did not apply it in the manner or in the time that it was needed the most. God provides a wisdom manual; *Proverbs*, in the middle of the book that he wrote to guide our living, The Bible.

    If we as men would apply the knowledge we have at critical points or junctures in our life, we would be able to avoid trips and traps that the enemy has set for our Kingdom purpose. If I would have applied some of the principles that this book covers at the critical points in my life, there would have been acceleration toward purpose as opposed to drag and weight, in direct opposition of my purpose. My prayer is that anyone who applies these proverbial principles would move supernaturally faster toward their purpose.

How to Use This Book

Proverbial Principles for the Purposed Man is collection of principles that when applied correctly to everyone's, more specifically a man's life, will ensure they remain steadfast in the pursuit and acquisition of divine purpose. Each of the principles stands on its own and finds potential relevance in very specific places in our lives.

This book is best used as a long-term devotional guide, given proper time between the study of each principle to decipher, digest, discern, and deploy each principle into your individual pursuit of purpose. Coupled with constant prayer and self-examination, this book has the power to unlock the next level of what God has specifically designed you to do. The truths covered in this book have perpetual application and when applied wholeheartedly will always keep you in true pursuit of your kingdom purpose.

Principle #1 – Begin with Reverence

"The fear of the Lord is the beginning of knowledge: but fools despise wisdom and instruction." Proverbs 1:7 (NIV)

If we as individuals, more specifically men, are seeking to live a purposed life, it must begin with the simple fact that God, the one and only true God – Yahweh, is the beginning. Genesis 1 tells us of the creation and the only thing that IS, before anything else is created, is God whom then creates everything else. What a powerful and divine concept. The proverb this truth is based on, empowers the reader on where everything begins and again it begins with fearing, that most powerful and divine individual, God.

Let us clarify a few terms that will add understanding to the truth. Fearing the Lord is meant in an honorable way. Fear, as spoken of here in the text, is derived from the Hebrew word *Yir'ah* meaning respect, reverence, piety, thus this first truth is named Beginning with Reverence, because this is the basis for which the following truths will be based. Reverencing and respecting the true and living God and a deep understanding of that is where purposed living begins especially for the typical alpha male personality of beings.

A man that understands that he is not his own, nor is he the Supreme Being ever to have walked the face of the earth begets or creates knowledge of its own. Men, who desire to lead their household correctly, should hold fast to the fact that God owns his household; he is merely an Under-Shephard. An acknowledgement to the truth of this statement should engender reverence for the owner of the household.

The psalmist puts this well in Psalm 127, "Except the Lord builds the house, they labor in vain that build it: except the Lord keep the city, the watchman waketh but in vain." We can respect the earthly landlords of our homes but fail to respect the God that created the ground the home sits on, the house itself, the owner of the home, and the property company that upkeeps the home and this is dangerous if we want to see God continue to prosper us. I've used this example of the home because so many men feel that their sole purpose is locked up in their home, however, when you begin to fear and reverence God, establish a valuable meaningful relationship with him, and begin to discover who he is, he will begin to reveal who you are and the true purpose he's placed you here. You are not where you are on accident, rather everything that has happened to you is a part of the story God wants to reveal to you so you can tell others (Romans 8:28).

So, I challenge you, men, to begin your purposed walk, by understanding this walk starts and ends with HIM!! Let's take the journey of a Proverbial Purposed Walk!!

Principle #2 – Make a Conscious Effort to Avoid the Seductive

"Wisdom will save you also from the adulterous woman, from the wayward woman with her seductive words, who has left the partner of her youth and ignored the covenant she made before God. Surely her house leads down to death and her paths to the spirits of the dead. None who go to her return or attain the paths of life" Proverbs 2:16-19 (NIV)

Destiny or Death!! Men listen, because you have decided to acknowledge God, go for greatness, drive for destiny, and pursue purpose, the enemy will always attempt to use a spirit of seduction that appeals to your natural man in order to cause any sliver of distraction possible.

You may notice in life sometimes that when you were single, it seemed no one wanted you, but when you got married, they came out of the wood works. When you were walking everyday back and forth to work, you had no friends, but when you saved your money and got a new car, friends magically appeared. That's because a purposed man is an attractive man. Your purpose, anointing, calling, or gifting will naturally draw people, but we must be careful in discerning who is "for" us and who is *for* us!

There is a spirit attacking the children of God that appeals to your nature and calls for them to devote time in order to determine the outcome, often resulting in a destructive dead end. And for men... it is the "Strange" woman, sometimes referred to as Jezebel. A spirit that seeks to acquire control of whatever it can so that it can turn the heart of the man. Anything that can compete for what should be your undivided attention at pursuing God's purpose for you can fall under this adulterous, wayward, seductive woman.

Solomon, a man of great wisdom, power, riches, and wealth fell privy to this very spirit as it appealed to his flesh in that he, "loved many foreign women" (1 Kings 11:1). He writes this proverbial truth to us as purposed men today to tell us that our divine destiny should be our deliberate focus. Pursue Purpose! Solomon says use wisdom to avoid her and you will be saved, for she has abandoned that which she one loved, and abandoned her commitment to God himself. If she cannot remain committed to God, nor the one she has loved since her youth, there is no way that this seductive spirit, as good as it may look and or feel, can remain committed to you and more explicitly a *purpose pursuing you*! He says avoid her house for her house is on a street called death row and highway leading there is one of evil dead spirit, Hwy 666. Those who enter her house enter a dark abyss and never return because once you partake in seductive sin, and I mean some good flesh-pleasing, parent forbid, ill-advised sin, it is difficult to find a clear path out. "But THANKS be to God, who delivers me through Christ Jesus" (Romans 7:25).

If you make your residence, her residence, you will never return and in never returning you will miss the many blessings and manifestations of promises that God had intended for you. It takes a continued conscious effort to apply wisdom and avoid it. It is sly, it is slick, it is sneaky, and before you know it will have to you surrounded in its web.

Men, its destiny or death! The enemy is out for your destiny, make the conscious effort to see behind what you are really seeing and determine the true nature of the thing. If it only wants you, because of the temporal, tangible, external, or physical it may be the "strange" woman pulling you from purpose.

Principle #3 – Trust Dictates Trajectory

"Trust in the LORD with all your heart, and lean not on your own understanding; in all Your ways acknowledge Him; And He shall direct your paths." Proverbs 3:5-6 (NKJV)

Do not discount Trust! We as men discount the value of trust and often because we as MEN habitually violate it! Trust is of extreme value especially in light of the world we live in today. Trust is a strong firm belief in the reliability, truth, ability, or strength of someone or something. Trust, applied, is an individual's unrelenting belief in another person's; they love or care about, reliability or ability. It is frequently given from the beginning and because we, as men, violate it so quickly and regularly we attempt to bring the value of it down.

The truth is that the value of *trust* does not decrease because you do not know how to properly honor, respect, and value it. I stated this truth to express the weight that trust carries and when placed in the right being, can dictate how high and how far you go.

Solomon encourages us to place all of our trust in the Lord. He essentially says, have a strong belief in the reliability and ability of the Lord. Because God created you with purpose before you were birthed into this world, as he did for Jeremiah (Jeremiah 1:5), he is the one that knows exactly what that purpose is. In all his infinite wisdom and knowledge, God also is the only person that knows the route designed for you to take in order to reach that purpose.

Therefore, if we are going to get to purpose we are going to have to be led there by the only person who knows how to get there. Issues arise, because we develop our own purpose and attempt to set our own destinies. Then once we have the dream idea of "what we want to be when we grow up," whether it lines up with Gods purpose for me or not, we attempt to do everything within our own power to get there. But the bible states, that we have to walk toward purpose blindly placing our faith and our trust in God. (2 Corinthians 5:7; Prov. 3:5).

We as men have to stop trusting in our upbringing, our wealth, our education, our advanced degrees, our job security, our 401K, our Roth IRA's, our family, our friends, our therapists, our coaches, our spouses, our cars, our homes, or any other thing to define or validate our purpose. Rather, look unto the author and finisher of our faith, the God that creates and sustains us, the one who put purpose on the inside of us, and the one who knows best how to get us there.

Men, it's when our trust is in him, that he can pull us back like an arrow and release us on the line of trajectory that arrives us at our purpose and destiny according to the appropriate time. Do not rush this flight, do not attempt to circumvent this trip, do not try to jump through the loops, allow God to determine your course by trusting in him and he will set you on the flight plan tailor equipped for you!!

Principle #4 – Do Discipline!

"He will die because there is no discipline, and be lost because of his great stupidity." Proverbs 5:23 (CSB)

One of the most challenging concepts for us as men to embrace is discipline and all of its forms. In order for you to remain on the path of purpose, there must be a combination of corrective discipline and personal discipline. Men have a natural disdain toward "discipline" because we often feel it subjects us and strips us of the right, we feel we have, to be dominant, decisive, and driven. What we fail to realize is that this mentality, instinctive to the male species, frequently leads to us into being dominant and domineering, in other words very un-delightful!

Although discipline does make you a subject, as a submitted subject unto God you could never ever miss the mark as it relates to your purpose and subsequently your relationships, your job, your marriage, your children, your money, or your goals for success. Peter encourages us to humble (submit) ourselves, under the mighty hand of God and he will exalt (or lift) you up at the proper time (1 Peter 5:6, NASB). But is must come as a result of or willingness to endure discipline.

The writer lets us know that where there is no discipline two things will result, loss of direction and death. Discipline in the corrective form placed us in a position where God can adjust our character for our purpose and confirm us to his image for eternity. There are times that he will correct us through his voice which sounds amazingly like his word, the word of God.

This is one reason and devotion time is so essential to arriving at purpose. It is a time where God can deal with us in his own way. It shows that we are willing and submitted enough to endure loving discipline. Loving discipline you ask? Yes, loving discipline. The Bible says, "For the LORD disciplines those he loves" (Prov. 3:2, Hebrews 12:6). When we are corrected it is a sign that God loves us and has accepted us as his own. We must position ourselves to welcome discipline so that we do not error in our decision making in our pursuit of purpose.

There must also be a level of personal discipline. We must hold our own selves accountable to parameters that will produce life giving habits. Many of us have not walked into promise because we have not held ourselves to personal boundaries or limitations. We live an, "anything goes," lifestyle a sort of "you only live once," life that while possibly gratifying to the flesh for the moment, does not push us closer to purpose or sustain a pliable path to destiny.

Living without these self-invoked parameters simply leads to twofold death – spiritual separation from God and physical separation from this life. "For the wages of sin is death, but the gift of God is eternal life in Christ Jesus our Lord," (Rom. 6:23) A life without boundaries is a breeding ground for sin and transgression to fill it. It opens a door and invites in destruction to the God given purpose of your life. It makes it easier to sin. It makes it easier to continue in deception. It makes it easier to backslide. It makes it easier to do things that are in direct conflict with God and his word. These actions set up a separating road block between you and God. It separates the relational union you have with God, because darkness, evil, wickedness, or sin is incapable of being in the presence of God because he is a Holy, righteous, and just God.

For the man in pursuit of purpose, this is a huge deal. Purpose cannot be achieved in and under your own power. You need the aid and assistance of the being that created you and *knows* your purpose. If then, you are separated from him, you are separated from his guidance, wisdom, direction, and most importantly his presence. These are critical elements needed to achieve purpose and arguably inextricable from the acquisition of it.

Men, choose to "do" discipline! It is not a way of diminishing your manhood, it is a way of defining it. It helps to keep your path directed and corrected! It keeps devoted time to God, in fact devoted to Him. It prevents death to you, your destiny, your blessing, your process, your vision, your promise, and ultimately your purpose!

Principle #5 – Force Yourself to Remain "In-Gear"

"Idle hands make one poor, but diligent hands bring riches" Proverbs 10:4 (HCSB)

When teaching a brand-new driver how to handle a manual transmission in a vehicle, then entire goal of their initial process is to learn everything that they need to learn in order to arrive at first (1st) gear. First gear is the primary goal. It is difficult, it is hard, it is a challenging concept to grasp. "How do I balance between the clutch and the gas, so as to ease in to first?" I have to get to first!

Once the individual understands how to get into first gear, they will never have the difficulty of shifting gears again. They will be able to move from first to second, second to third and so on. It is at this point the driver feels the speed of progression. Often times they never want to remain idle again. Similarly, once an individual begins to make vast progression in the things of God, he or she will never want to remain idle again. "How do I balance life between the clutch and the gas, so as to shift my life in the gear of purpose?"

As a man in pursuit of purpose, there will come many things that will oppose your progression and if you allow those things to keep you in idle the enemy is successful. *Dying having not reached purpose is a victory for the enemy.* This is why it's so very important not to get stuck in a never-ending *idle* loop. Idle, in its action form, is defined as spending time doing nothing.

When used to describe the man on the path to purpose, it is an individual in a spiritual posture where they are avoiding work, are lethargic, lazy, and without effect or purpose. Simply put, pointless. This is where the enemy wants to keep men - in a pointless loop. He attempts, and is very successful, by constantly reminding them of all of their poor decisions, inadequacies, and shaded histories. A man's history, places and keeps him in an *"idle"* status much longer than any man should ever remain. The writer says, that being idle will cause one to be poor, but hard-working diligent hands will make one rich. He is writing not only in the natural, but also spiritually. Any man knows that if he wants to make riches and wealth he will have to commit himself to working hard day in and day out. He will need a solid fundamental education, have to pursue a good collegiate education, garner various types of experience, and work significant hours, days, months, or even years to reach the wealth he desires.

However, I believe he is also speaking to things of God. The man that remains idle, suggesting, the one who is not educating or progressing himself toward his divine purpose, will find himself often unfulfilled, unhappy, and indifferent toward his spiritual walk. However, the man that is preparing diligently for where God has destined him to go, not only will find natural riches, but a rewarding, joyous, accomplished walk with God.

Reality is, when you are a man and you have chosen to pursue purpose through Christ Jesus, the Bible tells us that, "old things pass away and that all things become new," (2 Cor. 5:17). When Christ really enters your life and you begin to understand what he has purposed you to do, you will find strength to break free from the bondage of your past. Christ has died for it, forgiven it, and forgotten it, so why are you still carrying it? We as men cannot allow the enemy to continue to deceive us into believing that we are inadequate.

The bottom line is you are not what you did, or even what you did not or were not able to do. You can start over, you can overcome, you can start now, you can shift into gear today! Turn your issues, your inadequacies, your concerns, your cares, your past, your poor decisions, your self-hate, your low self-esteem, and most importantly your future and purpose over to God! He has already worked everything out for you if you would simply surrender to him today.

Men, pick yourself up and get back to the grind. Ask God to help you break the endless loop of pointlessness. God told the Israelite people through Moses that, "it is He that gives you the power to create wealth," (Deuteronomy 8:18). He hands given you air to breathe, a mind to think, and hands to work. Create your wealth naturally! He has given you his inspired holy word, salvation free of charge, and a new mind, body, and life if you'll accept it. Create your wealth spiritually! He will take you to higher heights and deeper depths if you will simply shift gears. The sky is *not* the limit, God is....and HE has no limits! Shift into the gear of your purpose!

Principle #6 – Discover and Deploy Your Gift

"A man's gift makes room for him, and brings him before great men." Proverbs 18:16 (NKJV)

Your purpose is inevitably tied to your gift(s). Because, as we discovered earlier, God knows your purpose and what he designed you to be before he birthed you, he was able to equip you with essential gift(s) that you would need to be successful in fulfilling the entirety of your purpose. Many men have difficulty discovering their purpose often because they have difficulty discovering and honing their gifts. One key thing that many people fail to realize is that our spiritual gifts are quite like our natural gifts or abilities. In order to discover them we must be active.

When a child is young, he wants to be the next Michael Jordan or the next Tom Brady. He wants to be able to perform miraculous feats within the confines of the field of play. Whether it be on the court, on the field, or on the green, the many athletes that excel, even succeed, at *their* sport spent some years being active in other extracurricular activities so that they could not only determine what they had a natural apt for but also what they had no apt in at all. Some successful athletes, writers, and businessman would be able to tell you exactly what they are *good* at and what they are not. They know this information because they have spent years putting their hands to work in many things until they determined the intersection of their apt and their passion. At that intersecting point is where one realizes a gift that God has given them.

Our spiritual gifts work very similarly. God has an intended design for you and your gifts. It is perfect! However, you must be the one to seek him as to his plan and put your hands to work, serve, in the kingdom in order to determine what you have an apt for and what you do not. Sometimes determining our spiritual gifting comes by divine calling, by revelation, or by impartation, conversely, sometimes we discover our gifts through a sort of trial and error method. For example, you may have signed up to be a Sunday morning greeter before service as a part of the hospitality team, only to find out that greeting people as they come into service did not bring fulfillment. This was a trial and error and now you know that you do not have a passion to work as a part of the welcoming team. You can now move forward with attempting to serve in another area. Again, where you're apt, within the context of the kingdom, and your passion intersects is a solid sign of a spiritual gift from God.

Solomon writes that it is *that gift* that will make room for you and bring you before great men. Like any gift or talent, it must be worked. You do not become Lebron James overnight. Although he had an apt for basketball he spent years developing that gift. Similarly, we must put our effort into developing and honing the gift god gave to us. We must put it to use. Paul told Timothy, "Therefore I remind you to stir up the gift of God which is in you through the laying on of my hands," (2 Timothy 1:6). There must be a conscious effort to activate, utilize, work, stretch, and grow our gift. It simply can't be put in the hands of God. He put it in us to discover it, develop it, and deploy it! When we do that with a heart for God, door will begin to open. You will begin to see platforms for the utilization of the God-given gift. It will bring you before great men. It will provide opportunity that you would not have had. It will bring kingdom success and ultimately it will bring heavenly reward.

Men, discover and deploy your gift! It is essential to your purpose. When you discover it, don't sit on it, rather work it so that it develops. Use it to serve in your individual household, your local church, and your community. When you do and wholeheartedly do it as unto the Lord, you will see things begin to line up, doors open, and opportunities you could have never imagined.

Principle #7 – Correct Your Company

"Do not make friends with a hot-tempered person, do not associate with one easily angered, or you may learn their ways and get yourself ensnared" Proverbs 22:24-25 (NIV)

It has been commonly said, "show me your friends and I can tell you your character." Although not 100% accurate, your friends are a very good indicator of the type of person you really are. This is true partially because of the way that we as human beings are created and developed. God, in all of his infinite wisdom and knowledge, created us as human beings to be people who needed fellowship via relationship.

We can see this principle put into practice when God tells Adam, "it is not good for him to be alone," (Genesis 2:18). God states he will make a helper suitable for him and as a result God creates a female companion named subsequently named Eve. The underlying principle is that Adam could not accomplish all that God would have for him to accomplish, that Adam would not reach or fulfill the entirety of his destiny, that Adam could not *do life* without the creation and development of relationship. He would need relationship to push him to the next level.

That very same principle applies to us as men today, we need fellowship through relationship to thrust us to the next level. If you don't believe this principle and you feel you do not need relationship, examine one of the most extreme harshest levels of criminal punishment – solitary confinement. Why is this considered harsh and for some cruel and unusual? Simply because it separates you from fellowship through relationship, the very thing God created you to need, and in some cases long for, in order to continue along the path of purpose.

With that being said, the wisdom saying encourages us to correct our company. He essentially says if you are not around the right people, correct it and correct it quickly. We are not God; therefore, we do have the ability to change people. We can encourage, we can exhort, we can aid, but we cannot force change. Only God can. However, we do have to ability to change, or *correct*, our immediate circle of friends. The writer says don't make friends with those who are hot tempered or easily angered, this is because individuals that fall into this category bring about destruction.

The general law of friendship is that we often make room for and accept to the point of defense the character of those we have deemed our friends. This concept becomes inherently dangerous if we associate ourselves or befriend those who, by their actions and our defense of them, would draw us into contempt of sin.

If a good friend of yours is angry with someone, he or she will expect you to be angry with them as well because of the connection between you two. But this is the exact opposite of what God did and calls us to do. He intentionally befriended those who others defriended all because he was able to check or correct his company. If you are too long with someone who does not align with the character that God has called you to, you will soon align your character with theirs as opposed to coming into the character God has called you for.

Your friends and those whom you keep close to you must be consistent with the purpose, assignment, call, and character on your life. Friends who character is inconsistent with your kingdom purpose and all that it will require will divide your attention and your focus which will consequently enable you to be inconsistent with God and his work for you. We have to remain on the path and to ensure that we must have individuals around us that can help get us there.

Men, your friend circle is more important to your purpose than you may think. It was the faith of the men that plowed through the roof of an overcrowded house to bring their paralyzed friend to Jesus (Luke 5:17-26). They were the direct cause of his healing. Your friends must have the consistent character and resilience to bring you into your kingdom purpose. I you don't have friends that are currently operating in their purpose, correct your company, or you too will walk out of and not into purpose!

Principle #8 – Do Not Hate on Them

"Never envy evil people, but always respect the Lord. This will give you something to hope for that will not disappoint you." Proverbs 23:17-18 (ERV)

One of the biggest distractions and subsequent obstacles to the pursuit of purpose is other people. Take that statement any way you would like, however you must take it! Like discussed in earlier chapters, God created us for relationship with other people, however, in pursuit of purpose an individual must delineate between when a person has arrived on the scene to be a supporter or a separator; whether they have come to be a driver toward purpose or a distractor from purpose. Identifying this early on in a relationship will allow you to stay steadfast on the narrow path of purpose.

A significant tactic of the enemy is to send people who seem to have an interest in seeing you excel, aiding you in achieving, or pumping you into a purposeful perspective, but in reality, they have really been sent to be a reminder of an attitude or approach you, at one point in your life, use to have. It is because of this that I have come to understand Gods dealings with me individually. God is so God, that his matter and method of dealing with his creation is tailor made for the creation. That is why there are certain things that it seems like people around you can always get away with or narrowly escape from, but if you were to do it one time, the first time, you are caught red-handed and prosecuted to the highest extent.

Kids, I knew, would skip school, hang out all day playing NFL Madden and NBA 2K and never be brought into contempt for their actions, while if I said, "shoot," the teacher thought I said another *s-word*, I was promptly sent to the office and given three (3) days of In-School Suspension (ISS). It was never fair. It never seemed right. This is because God deals with individuals' actions, behaviors, characteristics, and transformation processes at a level that is conducive to arriving them at their purpose in full potential. God sometimes will intervene to save you from yourself. He will interject so that you do not talk, touch, think, or throw yourself out of a potential blessing he was trying to send your way.

It is very important to understand and accept this principle, otherwise you will think and feel like the Psalmist when he said, "For I envied the arrogant when I saw the prosperity of the wicked" (Psalm 73:3). Assuming this theology is a dangerous place to dwell in because this attitude of the wicked prospering and I, the righteousness of Christ, am suffering would suggest that God is unjust. Scripture declares that God is Just and that he will repay trouble to those who trouble you (2 Thessalonians 1:6). He is fair and he rains on all, the just and the unjust people. He will however one day come back as the Judge.

It is at this point that justice will be served to those who may have prospered here on earth, but did everything in their power to squander everlasting life and their eternal riches. God will judge the wicked and will pay every man according to their works. For this reason, the wisdom writer says, "Never envy evil people." He essentially is saying never desire to go back to what you once were. Never yearn for a former shell of yourself. If you envy or desire the position or place they are in then you are largely saying, "God you made a mistake." The things they have may be enticing. The places they can go and enjoy themselves may be attractive. The people they can continuously interact with may be seductive, but never desire to go back.

The wisdom writer is subtly encouraging the reader forward. Forward in the things of God. Forward in your relationships. Forward in your friendships. Forward in your ideas. Forward in your sanctification process. Forward in your deliverance. Forward in your book. Forward in your business. Forward in your purpose. FORWARD!

Men, we must continue to keep our eye off of other people, their progression, their progress, and their potential or lack thereof and keep our eye on the pursuit of our own tailor-made purpose. Never desire to go back to who God delivered us from being. Always look to progress forward reverencing, respecting, and revering the Lord. This is what will give us the hope of attaining. He who starts a good work in you will see it to completion, even unto the day of Jesus Christ (Philippians 1:6). Don't look back and hate on them because you are already *ahead* of them!

Principle #9 – Remember His Sovereignty

"The king's heart is in the hand of the Lord, Like the rivers of water; He turns it wherever He wishes." – Proverbs 21:1

One of the toughest lessons I, as a man, had to come to grips with was that despite how strong, intelligent, prosperous, or powerful I had become God is a sovereign God. Despite how successful my upbringing had been, how set for destiny my adolescent years had been, how hard I pushed myself to work in order to secure the mere opportunity to have a future, how many "right" decisions I thought I had made, God was still a sovereign God! Need I go on? God was, is, and will always be Sovereign.

Scripture states that, "in Him all things were created: things in heaven and on earth, visible and invisible, whether thrones or powers or rulers or authorities; all things have been created through him and for him," (Colossians 1:16). This simple, but powerful verse of scripture essentially says that over everything that exists, God has complete authority and control. Humbly put, God can do what he wants, with whom he wants, how he wants, why he wants, where he wants, and when he wants and there is very little, we as creation, can say about it. This is a hard pill to swallow, but on the path to pursing purpose a necessary lesson to learn.

Solomon, who writes Proverbs 21, no doubt is in a place where he is reflecting on his reign. His life had been destined for purpose. His father had found unprecedented favor with God being that he was a man, "after Gods own heart," (1 Sam 13:14). Because King David walked close to God, the Lord set a generational purpose for his bloodline. They were to have a seed sit on the throne forever.

God also had assigned the specific task to David of rebuilding the temple, but because of his disobedience, King Solomon, his heir, became the conduit of that task and purpose. Yes, King Solomon had become the wisest and the wealthiest king to ever grace Israel and yet, he cautions us against the Sovereignty of God. King

Solomon made the decision for nations, however takes time to remind us that God can invoke his *veto* power, so to speak, and cause anything under his authority to change. Solomon writes to us as men to ensure we understand that at the end of it all, God still has the ability to overrule.

This concept does not just apply to decisions we make but even to the very intimate circumstances of our life. The parents we are born to, the color of our skin, our genetically make up, our mental capacity, our provision, and even our purpose – all a very sovereign decision from the creator and sustainer of all.

I learned and submitted to this lesson form a place in my life where there was no other option. God had allowed my situation, as a result of my decision making, to stoop so low that it felt as if the bottom had fallen out and there was never going to be a return. It was then God reminded me, that I was not supposed to be where I was, nonetheless, my life belonged to him and he would do or allow whatever he had to do or allow to ensure He got it back. The harsh reality is that remaining on the path to purpose will force us into situations where tough decisions will have to be made. They often called this in college, "the hard right or the easier wrong." Regardless of the decision made, God is so much God that he knew which decision you would make, how it would affect your path to purpose, and begins to alter the minor future details so that in the end it will all work out for your good and his glory. When your heart is truly in his hand, he will turn it in order for you to make decisions that will lead down the path He needs you to go down in order to prepare you for the greater purpose he has for you.

    NO matter where you find yourself currently know that greater is the end of a thing than the beginning (Ecclesiastes 7:8) and he that has begun a good work in you will perform it until Christ returns (Philippians 1:6). Therefore, nothing can stop the sovereign hand of God, he is always attempting to build you up to greater and will continue to do it, in spite of how your immediate circumstances look, until the end of time.

Men, God has the ability to shift any situation, problem, or concern in your favor. His sovereignty is unmatched and unparalleled. Without a doubt he has complete control over every single detail concerning your life. Keep your heart near his! Keep your trust in Gods heart, even when you can't trace his hand. He will perfect that which concerns you (Psalm 138:8).

Principle #10 – Show Honor

"Whoever oppresses the poor shows contempt for their Maker, but whoever is kind to the needy honors God." - Proverbs 14:31 (NIV)

You must show honor to whom honor is due, however, you must show honor to those who you feel are unworthy of your honor. Society, in the twenty-first century, has warped people into a distorted sense of both giving and receiving honor. We begin to feel as if people who have attained a specific level of status, power, position, or prominence are the only individuals who are honor-worthy.

    We are easily able to speak highly of those in political position or those who have made a significant impact on the history of our country or our culture, but we have difficulty finding positive words to speak about the person that lives down the street who constantly sits on his or her porch to wave at people that go by, day after day. Why? It is because we have an inaccurate view of how God intended us as individuals to interact with Him and with each other.

To fully understand this principle, you must review how each and every individual was created. Moses gives us this account in the book of Genesis. God said, "Let us make mankind in our image and in our likeness," (Gen1:26). He goes on to say, it was in his very image that he created male and female as a spirit. This is an important note because he shows us that in order to find out who someone truly is you must look beyond the casing they have been placed in. God places the spirit in a *body,* or housing so to speak, in Genesis 2:7 and that is what places the limitations, characteristics, features, and personal details on the spirit.

Unfortunately, these very limitations and characteristics are what people use to determine the level of honor, if any, an individual should receive. Determining honor via this process is a very carnal way to live. God intended for us, by way of the Holy Spirit, to be able to utilize the spirit of discernment to see beyond what we physically see. More specifically, to be able to see the very root or nature of a thing. It is by this that we should see a person how God sees a person.

By applying this important observation, the proverbial writer shows us in this particular verse that we display our honor for God by how we honor his creation. How you handle the things that are nearest and dearest to Gods heart is an accurate indication of how your heart is postured toward God. Solomon says if you oppress intentionality in ensuring hardship or subservient status – those who already, for whatever reason, find them self in a substandard way of life, then you show God you have no regard for his heart or Him. He is essentially saying if you go out of your way to avoid or ignore a situation with his creation where you could otherwise place value, then you diminish value. There is no middle ground.

Conversely, if you do all that you can, in every situation that arrives in the arena of your life, to add value, you express to God you have a heart for his people and that your heart is postured toward Him. This is an exhortation to extend to others what they cannot extend in return. A cursory read of this would imply that you should live by the modern-day *golden rule* - to treat others as you would like to be treated, however Christ encouraged us to treat others like God treats us. Solomon's statement here in Proverbs prefaces and echoes the words of Christ, do all that you can to add value regardless of all circumstances. In this you bring God honor.

In pursuit of the path of purpose, honor is an essential ingredient in arriving on time and sustaining the effectiveness of your purpose. An example of this is those who dishonor those around them in order to achieve a preferred status or position. They arrive at the top, a higher level position or role, early and often find their time there is short-lived all because they dishonored to get there. Arriving early – not in Gods timing - at purpose allows you to arrive at the blessing unprepared. There is great danger in arriving at the blessing of God unprepared for the entirety of it. You often will make ill-advised decisions and poor choices in addition to not internalizing the passion and drive it requires to remain successful within the blessing. There is also the very real element of those whom you have dishonored having to be the very people you must now depend on and now as a result of the dishonor you have sown, dishonor and disrespect you will reap.

Those individuals will often do all that they can to ensure you are not permanently sustained in that respective position. Your blessing will be forfeited because you dishonored to acquire it. In purpose our entire goal should be to honor God while bringing, showing, and pointing people toward Gods glory.

Men, be extremely careful in how you receive and show honor. Honor coming in and honor going out. Honor even in the transition seasons of your life. When you feel good, honor, when you don't feel like it, show honor. There will be times that your flesh will make you feel as if someone does not deserve your honor, overrule your flesh with the spirit and see the very nature of that person to show them honor!!

When you show honor, you show that you can be trusted with the blessing, the future life, and the purpose God has in store for you.

A Prayer for Purpose

Heavenly Father,

I pray now for a deeper revelation of the identity and the purpose that you have for my life. I admit that I have a personal preference for my life, but because I know you have a plan that is easier and greater than mine, I lay down my will so that your will can be done in my life in accordance with **Luke 22:42**. I begin today to create an atmosphere conducive to hearing you through your audible voice and through your written word.

    I prophetically decree that this is the day that you begin to shift me toward my uniquely designed purpose. I pray that you allow my purpose to consume me. I pray for a passion to pursue it relentlessly and that in my pursuit and acquirement of it, I would bring you ultimate glory and honor. I pray that this is the day you begin to display your hand in my life as it relates to my purpose.

God, I ask that you would release the opportunities and the resources that I need to be successful in purpose. Every financial hindrance that is blocking me from overflow, I command it to be broken now in the name of Jesus. Give me the proper habits and skill I need now in order to sustain purpose in my life.

Today, I take my rightful spiritual place in purpose. Everywhere the sole of my feet tread shall be mine according to **Joshua 1:3**, everything that my hands touch shall be according to **Deuteronomy 30:9**. Today I speak purpose over my life and that purpose shall make me rich and add no sorrow in accordance with **Proverbs 10:22**. I declare that no weapon formed against me or my purpose shall prosper according to **Isaiah 54:17**.

Thank you, Lord, for purpose, position, power, provision, prestige, and promise in my life! I walk in this new season today! In the name of the Lord Jesus Christ, **Amen!**

CPSIA information can be obtained
at www.ICGtesting.com
Printed in the USA
LVHW110046291019
635548LV00004B/1154/P